LAUGH OUT LOUD

I RUFF JOKES

I don't!

By Jeffrey Burton

LITTLE SIMON

New York   London   Toronto   Sydney   New Delhi

LITTLE SIMON
An imprint of Simon & Schuster Children's Publishing Division
1230 Avenue of the Americas, New York, New York 10020
First Little Simon edition September 2017
Text copyright © 2017 by Simon & Schuster, Inc.
Photographs copyright © 2017 by Thinkstock. All rights reserved.
For information about special discounts for bulk purchases, please contact Simon & Schuster Special Sales at
1-866-506-1949 or business@simonandschuster.com.
The Simon & Schuster Speakers Bureau can bring authors to your live event. For more information or to book an event
contact the Simon & Schuster Speakers Bureau at 1-866-248-3049 or visit our website at www.simonspeakers.com.
Designed by Brittany Naundorff
Manufactured in China 0617 QUL
10 9 8 7 6 5 4 3 2 1
ISBN 978-1-5344-0029-0
ISBN 978-1-5344-0030-6 (eBook)

Welcome and get ready to LAUGH OUT LOUD
with this Animal Meme Joke Book that's out to prove once
and for all that wildlife are the funniest critters on earth.

Before you start, here are some helpful tips to make this
book even funnier:

- give each animal its own special voice
- give each joke its own special delivery
- make sure you share the best jokes with your friends
- and don't be afraid to make up your own jokes, too!

Hey! I know a great knock-knock joke. You start.

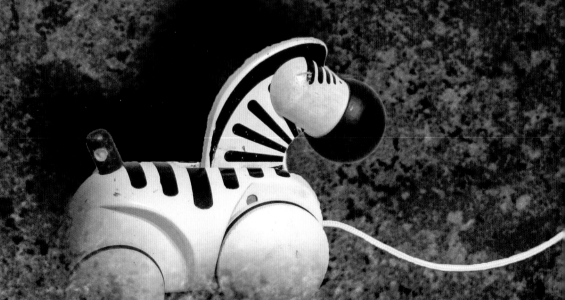

FINE! IF YOU'RE GOING
TO BE THAT WAY,

I'M TAKING MY TOY AND GOING **HOME**.

NUTS?

NUTS!

NUTS?

This hat looked bigger in the store...

WHEN YOUR DAD EATS THE LAST COOKIE.

OH MEOW GOSH, THE BALL HAS A BELL INSIDE!

BAD
SELFIE.

WELL, THIS IS ANOTHER FINE MESS YOU'VE GOTTEN YOURSELF INTO, NIBBLES.

Hi, I'm Sweetums.
I like eating scraps off the floor and chewing on dirty socks.

The secret password is . . .

doodles.

NO, REALLY. TELL MORE CAT JOKES. I LOVE CAT JOKES.

we're out of tea.

I BELIEVE THE WORD YOU'RE LOOKING FOR IS ADORABLE.

WHEN YOU'RE AT SCHOOL
AND YOU SEE OTHER KIDS OUTSIDE.

CAT,

CATTER,
CATTEST.

Here comes Hamster Claus.

Here comes Hamster Claus.

Right down Hamster Claus Lane.

SMILE!!

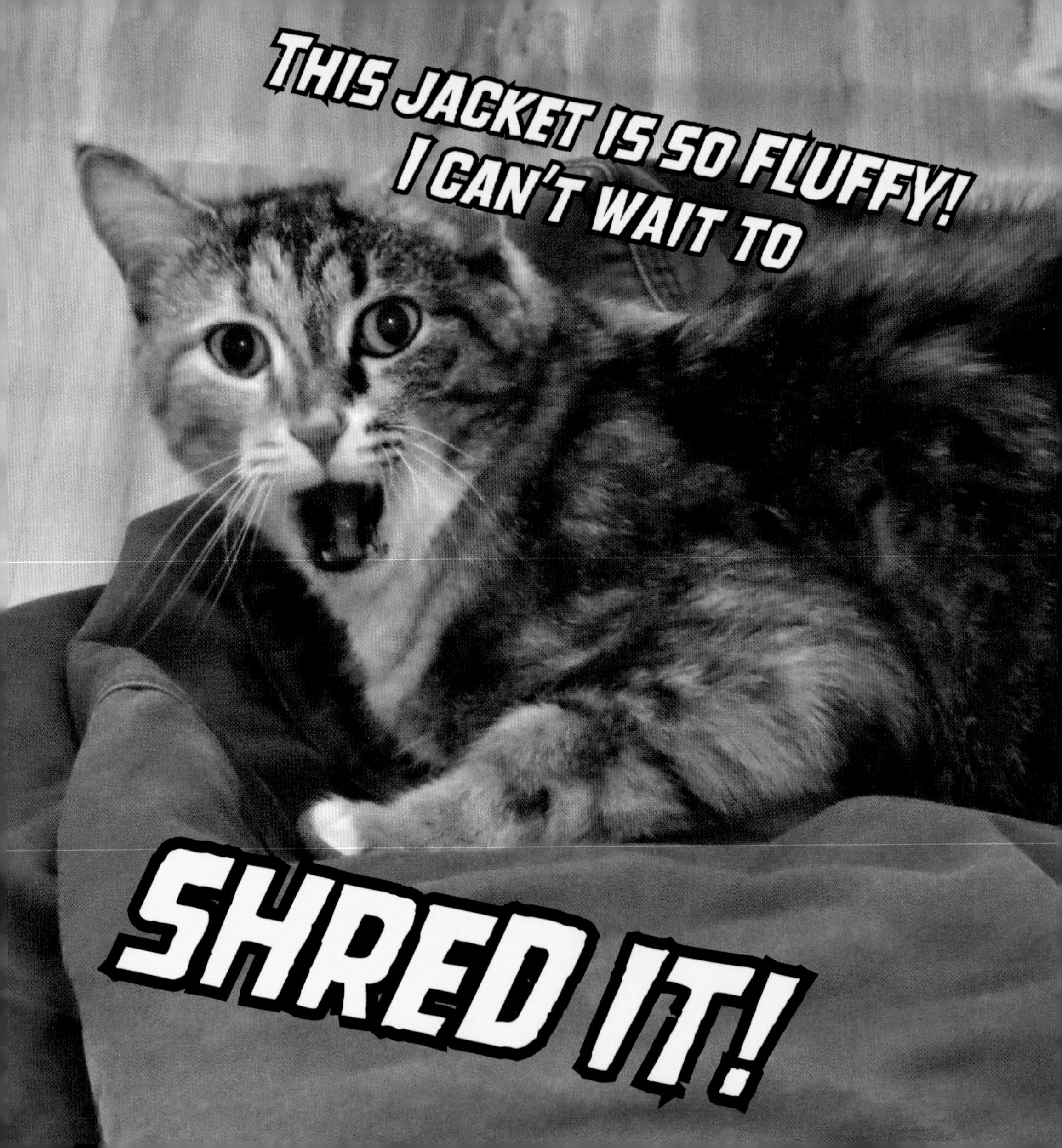
THIS JACKET IS SO FLUFFY!
I CAN'T WAIT TO
SHRED IT!

One is the loneliest number . . .
I've done the math.

When kids go to school and I'm like, don't mind me, I'm just gonna play with your toys all day.

We meet again, Mr. Duck.

WHEN YOU GET THE JOKE 15 MINUTES LATER.

When Ralphy tries to look happy,

but he knows your pizza is better than his dog food.

THE MAGIC CAT WILL
SEE YOU NOW.

SOCIAL MEOW-DIA

Want bonus homework?

NEVER CHALLENGE THIS GUY TO A PUSH-UP BATTLE.

can you believe this weather?

OH
GREAT.
I'M STUCK.

Moo! Moo!

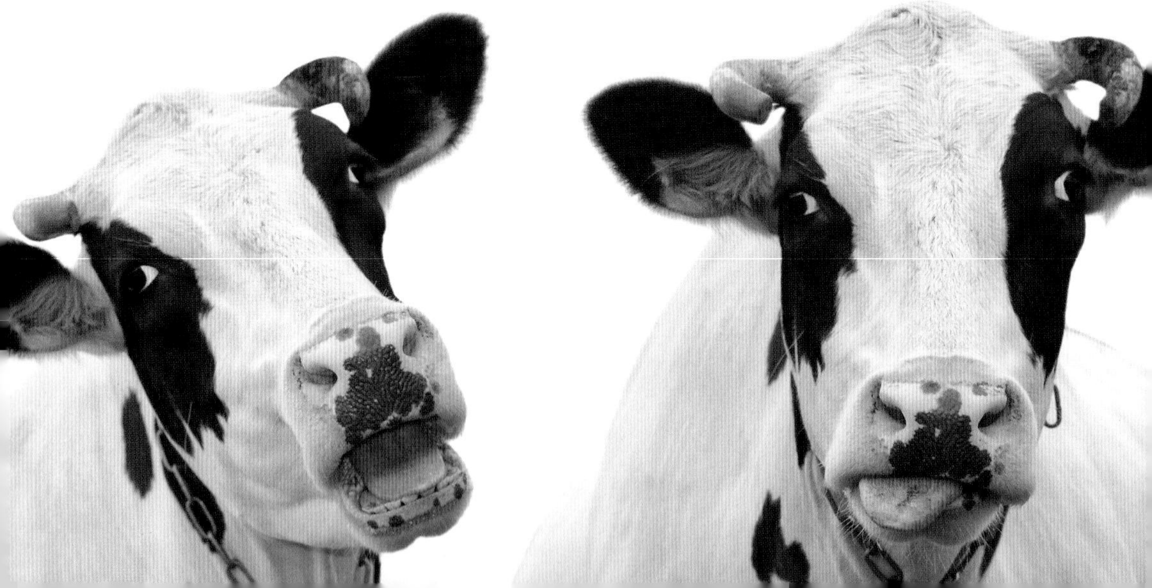

I told you, I'm not singing.

Quit showing off, yoga master.

AS A MATTER OF FACT, I **WAS** RAISED IN THE WOODS.

MEANWHILE, AT THE CAT OLYMPICS . . .

Why is the whole world
upside down?

Mittens dares you

to wash your hands.

NO, I MEAN, IT LOOKS GOOD . . .
ON YOU.

When mom insists you go to the school dance.

No one

can see me

because I'm

camel-flaged.

I heard you wanted to
PLAY!

'Twas I who stole the  from the COOKiE JAR!

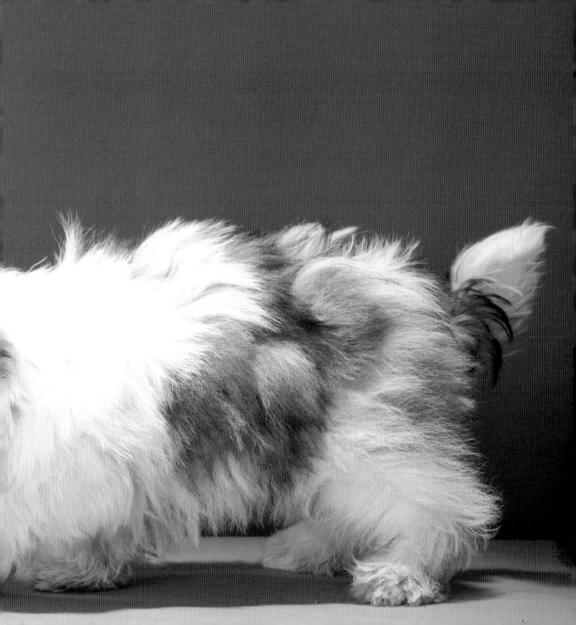

SOMETHING SMELLS FUNNY.

NEXT STOP:
ADVENTURE!

When you
think
there's a
ghost

behind
you.

MONKEY FACT:
Anyone who smiles this much
has a secret. *A deep, dark secret.*

THE CAT KNOWS WHEN IT'S TIME TO WAKE UP, HUMAN.

Well, the password's not my name . . .

Cat-tastic Dance Party!

Someone bRoke

kitty balleRina.

Just another day at the beach.

THE LEMUR KNOWS WHAT YOU DID.

Horse hats optional.

the square root of cute and fluffy is animals in glasses.

My face
when people
miss me in
dodgeball.

I'M READY FOR THE MARCH OF THE PENGUINS.

Hmmm, the stock market is going **bananas.**

The lifeguard is

on duty.

Is this a toy or is it a TRap?

THIS WAS A BAD IDEA.

When your present is smaller than what you asked for.

MEET THE DREADED PARROT BLUEBIRD. SCOURGE OF THE ANIMAL ENCLOSURE AT THE ZOO.

Pardon me.
Might you spare a

WHEN YOU FORGET YOUR LINES IN THE SCHOOL PLAY.

We're going to the future, Marty.

what was in that snail I ate?

WAITING FOR DAD TO PUT DOWN THE TV REMOTE.

MADE OF CUTE NIGHTMARES.

I KNOW YOU DON'T LIKE ME SCRATCHING THE SOFA.
I JUST DON'T CARE.

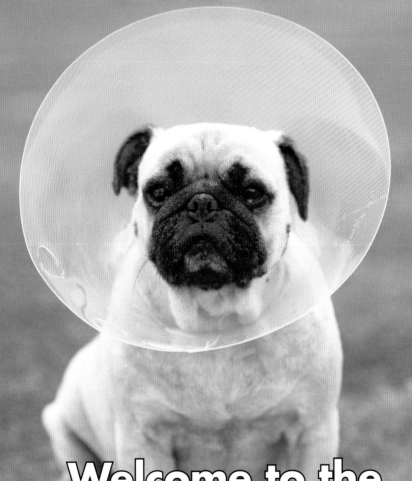

Welcome to the

CONE OF SHAME.

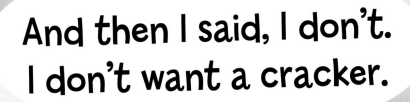

One time I found
a rock that looked
exactly like me.
I named him Rocky.

CAT REALIZES THAT SHE IS ALONE IN THE HOUSE.

The moment before your friend scares you to death.

WHEN YOUR LITTLE SISTER
TRIES TO TELL A JOKE.

I've come to
gRant you
thRee wishes—
**no more,
no less.**

Runner-up in the sadness contest.

Sea lion IS NOT impressed.

Reading is **groovy, baby.** But so is walking your dog.

Change the channel, or I'm
PULLING THE PLUG!

whoa, it worked.

ARE YOU . . .
LICKING MY BACK?
DON'T DO THAT.
THAT'S WEIRD.

Throw me the ball! I'm open! I'm open!!

WHAT ANIMALS DREAM ABOUT.

Is that allowed in soccer?

WOLFDOG KNOWS
WHAT YOU DID.

WHEN YOUR BROTHER GETS THE SAME TOY AS YOU.

MEANWHILE, AT THE CAT OLYMPICS . . .

NATURE SMELLS

SO NATURE-Y.

Don't worry. I goat your back.

I don't got this.

Hey! Socks just busted through a brick wall.

THE MOMENT YOU GET TOO BIG FOR YOUR BRITCHES.

Let's hear what Professor Barkley has to say.

LEVITATE POWER!

WHEN YOUR SISTER ALSO
GETS TO STAY UP LATE.

this little monkey toe went to the market . . .

Hello. So, do you

HANG AROUND HERE

often?

MAXIN' and Relaxin'

Hey!
You found me!

Don't
CHANGE THE
STATION WHEN
MY SONG IS ON.

WHEN YOU TELL YOUR FRIENDS YOU DON'T LIKE THEIR FAVORITE BOOK.

SPOT REALIZES HE'S BEEN CHASING HIS OWN TAIL ALL ALONG.

IT'S A CUPCAKE, CARL!
A SINGLE CUPCAKE!

EVERY FRIDAY AFTER SCHOOL, KIDS BE LIKE

NOT IMPRESSED.

Hot dogs

with

hORSeRadish?

GROSS!

Mouse secret: I took all the bad selfie pictures.